Small Talk

poems by

Jeffrey Schwartz

Finishing Line Press
Georgetown, Kentucky

Small Talk

Copyright © 2025 by Jeffrey Schwartz
ISBN 979-8-89990-134-8 First Edition
All rights reserved under International and Pan-American Copyright Conventions. No part of this book may be reproduced in any manner whatsoever without written permission from the publisher, except in the case of brief quotations embodied in critical articles and reviews.

ACKNOWLEDGMENTS

Thanks to the editors of the following publications where some of these poems originally appeared:

Abandoned Mine: The First Time I Contemplated Eternity; The Joy of Aging
Connecticut Literary Anthology: The Singer Machine
English Journal: Lockdown
Hanging Loose: Volver; The Weight
The Jewish Poets Collective Journal: Postcard from the Coast
Naugatuck River Review: Lee Road Accident
Paterson Literary Review: Angels on Elevators; Mary Mary
Pedestal Magazine: Saturday Morning, Beach 3
Porter Gulch: Time
Snapdragon: Ulysses Returns to the Suburbs

Publisher: Leah Huete de Maines
Editor: Christen Kincaid
Cover Art: "Follow the Lightning" by Kelly Knight © Kelly Knight 2024
Author Photo: Courtesy of Global Online Academy
Cover Design: Elizabeth Maines McCleavy

Order online: www.finishinglinepress.com
also available on amazon.com

Author inquiries and mail orders:
Finishing Line Press
PO Box 1626
Georgetown, Kentucky 40324
USA

Contents

I know what it's like 1

The Open Field 2

Ulysses Returns to the Suburbs 4

Circe's Hawk 5

Saturday Morning, Beach 3 6

Somewhere Under the Hudson 7

Mary, Mary 8

Reserved Seat, Ocean View 11

The Singer Machine 13

The Joy of Aging 14

The first time I contemplated eternity 15

Time 16

Ice & Fire 18

Volver 19

Small Talk 20

Believe It 21

Lightning Sonnet 22

Lee Road Accident 23

Lockdown 25

Cross-Continental Calls 26

Bread & Air 27

God's Rules 28

Angels on Escalators 29

The Weight 30

Postcard from the Coast 32

*for Diane & Dave
& in memory of our parents*

I know what it's like

to be dead, my 95-year-old dad said
halfway through the usual complaints

& staticky silences. Anger
& impatience dissolved like a pair

of chalky tablets in a tall glass
of milky water. Drink it, someone told

me once, & I did. Usually, it takes a minute
for him to talk into the phone after he fishes it

from his pocket & another minute to turn down
the TV stuck on football. Astounded,

I tried to drink it in. What do you mean by
dead, I asked, fearing the final rehearsal of

what lies ahead. I sat in my chair awake,
all night, my father said, right where the aide

found me this morning. What the hell are you doing
there, she asked. And then, he said,

she helped me undress & get into bed. I wasn't
anxious. I never needed to piss. I actually

felt calm. I knew I was going to die in my chair
with the TV on, not paying attention. Not caring

if you'd call, but kind of wishing you would.
At that moment, I felt his heart pounding

in my chest. And then the static returned
& my cell lost its signal. And then silence.

The Open Field

> *Out beyond ideas of wrongdoing and rightdoing,*
> *there is a field. I'll meet you there.* —Rumi

I look up at the screen to see an aged face among 300 windows
at a virtual poetry gathering. He looks a little hunched, his gray goatee

wild & untamed & in his shirt pocket, a carrying case for his glasses.
Recovering from a pre-virus stroke, he has to be reminded by a poet

in the Zoom window above him what they planned for him to read.
It is Rumi, of course, whom he introduced to the Western world,

Rumi who rings even truer when we fear losing ourselves
& what matters. Now when rightdoing is more on our minds

than before, we expect isolation in the field, a full six feet or more
from the touch of others. After he reads, the poet removes his glasses,

looks directly at me in my screen, swivels in his chair, & disappears
from his desk, leaving the computer camera staring at an empty room.

Even the bookcases are disheveled & the natural light is blocked
by a gauzy blue drape hung haphazardly over the back window.

What does it mean—to meet in a field beyond wrongdoing and
    rightdoing?
Where does the wise man go when he moves away from his screen?

In a previous world where we thought nothing we did contaminated
another, were we as separate as we supposed? I wait in a crooked,
    chaotic line

on the sidewalk & in the handicap spaces in front of A&S for a limited,
over-priced box of groceries. Some of us wear masks, some don't.

We haven't learned yet to calculate distance vs intimacy like the doctors
at Mount Sinai who double their protection with plastic shields

between their lips & the lips of their patients, many of whom are so
   sedated
they don't hear the doctor introduce herself & share what she's going
   to do next:

turn you on your belly because even though you might not think so,
   it's easier
on the lungs. They've checked your vitals & your DNR request &
   next will gently

shift the breathing tube in the ventilator so you don't develop an
   ulcer.
Once at the end of her shift, one of the pulmonologist's colleagues
   catered

an Italian dinner for the entire ICU team. For five minutes, there
   were no blinking
lights over doorways, no patient alarms on the monitor—pure luck—
   so they could

enjoy their meal of ragu with sweet sausage on paper plates.
No wine, no talk. But in those days, a "love you" before they depart.

Ulysses Returns to the Suburbs

We could always tell by the beard
that he had let loose with the guys

in the wilds of Canada, that he had
caught more fish than he could eat

& spent the evenings, probably, swearing
& drinking to proportions we only saw

at home football games in Cleveland
when the temps fell way below zero.

At Judd Tooley's the lake froze early & so solid,
that ice, packed in sawdust, lasted in blocks

the whole summer. Until Tooley's, he told us, no one
knew where to fish, how to clean & cook their catch,

or even start a fire. They slept better. Their appetites grew.
Fishing till dark gave them time to get lost, to unlearn

the calendar, to forage & quarrel according to their natures.
They survived thunderstorms, bad singing, & one-eyed

creatures that spooked them in the night. The night he sailed
home in his luminous Chrysler convertible, the dog knew him first.

Circe's Hawk

Had it landed a branch lower, I could
have touched the soft belly of the hawk

before it turned its back, as if fastening
a cloak barely wide enough to reach

around its broad shoulders. Willing it to stay,
I grip the limbs of the aluminum lawn chair

and scour the garden with a hawk's eye for
chipmunks scavenging among the purple Angelonia

and expired daylilies. Circe, too, landed
suddenly in nature—condemned to an island

she tamed to suit her magical needs. Every herb
became a potion strong enough to turn

sailors into swine. And back to men. With his permission,
she once clipped the venomous tail from Trygon to save

her son, half-mortal. She was willing to give her
own life to pay the price. In the cedar

a few yards from where I sit, the red-tailed hawk
arranges & rearranges its feathered cloak

as if to say, Dare you. Dare you
to find words to name what you see, & when I do,

the hawk slowly swivels its head, showing off its
terrifying beak. Reach, it beckons. Stroke these feathers

to feel if there's a man inside. Or, because
I am neither quick nor brave: Follow. Follow.

Saturday Morning, Beach 3

At the end of the street, we can see rescue teams
from other towns & firemen carrying oxygen tanks

across our neighbor's lawn. In this sleepy village, toddlers
take their first steps at this lake. Lovers paddle at twilight

in tilt-proof canoes. Kids learn to cast their lines off the dock.
From a kayak you can't see the bottom but if you're lucky,

a snake will slither past or you'll spot a box turtle sunning
itself on a half-submerged log. The waters are quietest

at this hour before families gather. Never these sirens
& flashing lights, never this anguish as palpable

as morning fog. From the raised porch, I can see
yellow tape cordon off the beach where I sat last night

with Jessie staring at the calm. Moira pushes a toy lawnmower
up the cul de sac & the neighbor whose husband is recovering

from Covid walks slowly down her driveway to ask
if what she heard was true. Channel 12 will confirm it

with shots of our lake and the diving crews. Even
when they find the body 50 feet offshore in 5 feet of water

no one can say how this happened. When little kids release
a fish back into the lake, they grip its slippery scales,

stare at its pulsing mouth & then lower the fish to the surface
where they watch it curl like a question mark & disappear.

Somewhere Under the Hudson

after Fellini

Sometimes I feel like I'm trapped in my car
in a tunnel & when I panic, pounding

on the windows, others in their automobiles
gawk vacantly or go on with the business of

crosswords, karaoke, TikTok, or simply breathing
with meditation apps on illumined phones. For some

that works, glass behind glass under a roiling
river. They don't think about the river or

the contamination creeping through the AC.
The only escape is through the sunroof

where I drift kite-like into a cloudless sky.
From this vantage I can see Manhattan

& Jersey, including the beach where
I'll safely land. My mother will be there

& Aunt Mildred & all the rest who used
to promenade along the boardwalk in Asbury Park.

The bullet that went through Louis's brain
will reverse into the handgun hidden in a basement

drawer. But I won't even think about that.
As a matter of fact, I feel like tapdancing

down a hallway where either love
or trouble waits behind a hotel door.

Mary, Mary

1.
Your last week on earth
the century's worst storm hit the East Coast,
the river you couldn't see from your window
spilled over its banks flooding
up to second floors & ricocheting boats in their basins,
Ocean Avenue disappeared under three feet of sand,
& no one was allowed home to Sea Bright
without an escort from the National Guard.

2.
It's hard to detach. You left us
Post-its in books, reminders by the phone,
annotations on newspapers you couldn't
throw out. Everywhere, hand-written notes.

The first time we left Ben with you at the shore,
you wrote a minute-by-minute journal
to humor my insecurity. "Listen," you tried to assure me.
"When I was only 13, I took care of every Catholic
kid in The Port." I got it: people trusted you,
people loved you. You created lasting connections
effortlessly. By the time you reached the register,
you knew the life stories of people buying groceries.
You bonded equally with your nurses & hairdresser,
your Club Girls from elementary school,
your neighbors in London & Toronto & all over Jersey,
the woman who cleaned the condo, my relatives (who also
grew up along the Shore), & even the Fed Ex man
who appeared in uniform at your wake.

3.
A week before, when there was still no power, a bunch of us
sat around the dining room table lit by two elegant candelabra,
emptying Dave's case of Southern Hemisphere wine & swapping
    family stories

like how your mother, Margaret, escorted her sister across the
    Atlantic
only to arrive at Ellis Island with no one to greet them.
Shortly after, they appeared in Elizabethport before relatives
who opened their door in shock, crying, "Jesus, Mary, and Joseph!
How did you find your way?" to which Margaret calmly replied,
"Ah, sure, do you think we have no maps in Ireland?"

4.
                                    Before you were married,
you worked as a receptionist at Esso & saved dollars to take
the boat to see your mother's family in County Clare.
They didn't know what to make of you, a young woman
with fiery red hair who loved to dance, their sister Margaret's
daughter, appearing with a suitcase full of gifts.

You stayed in the family house, the one with the thatched roof
heated by sod, which was enough. Simple was always enough.
So when the storm came to New Jersey, the biggest hurricane
anyone had ever seen, it hardly mattered because you
were perfectly comfortable in the hospital along the Navesink
pulsing on back-up power. "Why are people visiting me?"
you asked. "Am I sick?" "Am I dying?" And later, "Well, if I'm dying,
let's clean this place." I see you sitting up in the bed
you died in four days later, applying lipstick. That was the day
you spoke to Ben on the phone & Dennis visited. Clearly,
you touched them. And they touched you. Were you always
unafraid to express your love?

5.
The last day you were lucid, you had your daughter bring Patty's
cellophane-wrapped bags of chocolate pretzels to give to the nurses
at Riverview. In your last call with Dr. Konnor, the one
where he was supposed to tell you that the cancer was spreading
too rapidly & that the treatments now could only be "palliative,"
the good doctor never got a word in, because you spent the call
thanking him & sending your love to Amy who was just married

and Katrina who just had a baby & all the others who attended you
the last six years at Sloan Kettering. Despite the nightmarish pain,
you seemed ready to cede control. You asked
for a priest & then joked about keeping him waiting.

6.
Somewhere in the Caribbean, just before midnight, the music paused,
the lights dimmed, Betsy & I in black gown & tux, looked up
three stories from the dance floor, & there you were,
perfectly balanced, somehow the first one to pour atop a pyramid
of champagne glasses. And at the ring of the new year,
far, far from New York & the turmoil of the next decade, the emcee
at the microphone announced the first to bring in 2002
would be Mary. Mary from New Jersey.

7.
Last night I had a dream that I needed to save the Queen
of England & she was aging & close to death so it seemed
a bit futile but nevertheless my duty or at least the mechanism
to keep the story going, & at the moment when it all seemed over,
you, I mean the Queen, created a diversion & jumped over the side
of the boat. And all I could do was follow. Into the sea. To make sure
no one would harm you. You were playing in the waves
& then you were safe in your castle & you had out-smarted them
& survived & now, alongside your family, you could re-take your throne.

Reserved Seat, Ocean View

It was a simple goal.
If ever I returned to Florida

I'd order a frozen drink
at an outdoor bar.

I'd pull up a stool
next to my grandfather

who has been waiting
decades for me to find him.

Mango's best, he advises,
though he's never tried one himself

so I order mango
& we talk about his 65th reunion

how many of his buddies
are still alive

which ones flew in from out of state
& who still lives in Miami.

He tells me about some cousin
he hasn't seen since she was 8

who's staying at his place with her boyfriend
which, I admit, makes me a bit jealous.

I can't quite imagine them
in the tiny house we used to visit

especially with his eyesight
the way it is now, legally blind,

or how he'll show them the videos
he rattles off—when I knew him

videos weren't even invented
& I can't remember his ever watching TV

except to yell back at the newscasters.
What happened to Grandma, I ask,

and the Farias across the street?
Whatever happened to the banyan tree

you propped up after the hurricane of '66
and your prized coconuts and avocados?

Did you keep painting? And how do you cope
without a car? As a matter of fact,

how did you get here—to the Splash Bar—
30 years since I saw you last?

He looks as tanned and healthy as
that summer we delivered his sister

to a retirement home, now a brightly painted
hotel in fashionable South Beach

where he joked about the sad state
of the elderly.

Tonight he's tickled by the sight
of gray in my hair

& asks about his great-grandson
who has never seen

palm trees sway quite like these
under a ripening Florida-orange moon.

The Singer Machine

Diane sends me the photo
of our grandmother's sewing machine
crouched in a corner, polished black
with gold Singer script & silver throat plate,
circa 1933. She's cleaning the house
for a stager in Cleveland who won't
let anything stay as it is. The dining room
(formerly Peach) has to be painted Smoke Tan.
The 60s record cabinet has to be pitched.
Diane's gorgeous oak desk must go.
What a mess! And those plants—
twenty years of intimate care—
they block the window. Clutter's
the enemy for prospective buyers
who will want to imagine
their own stuff in an empty
house. But not too empty or
it'll feel abandoned. And there
are already too many of those
in Cleveland. The question is
where to hide the sewing machine
& those boxes of family papers, stained
with the smoke of personal history.
Our grandmother ran into a fire
to save that machine. It was
the only thing she couldn't let go.

The Joy of Aging

They get it. The way the word *detritus*
opens their mouths and lands on a sibilant 's'

& how it lifts them to family attics
full of old dinnerware, dolls with yarn hair, & knickknacks

their adult children someday will discard.
They feel the endurance

it takes to recite a 3-stanza long sentence as it empties
their lungs. And they hang on to that last breath

because they suspect that even when they wish
that words will be enough, they know they will not.

And when we read the poem about the mother
flicking sunburn peels off her son's shoulders,

they can feel the hot flesh. They know
the touch of love and the reverse: the slow

compression of regret like tissue paper
flattened under wedding gifts that, decades

later, still ask to be unpacked. And when
we get to the poem about grief & letting

go, they recognize how death hits you
when the shopping bag breaks, or the spoon

jams the disposal, or the way you glimpse
your spouse's reflection not in the moment you're browsing

in front of the store window, but a fraction
of a second later, after you've passed.

with thanks to Hall, Hayden, Olds, & Howe

The first time I contemplated eternity

was in a Shaker cemetery in the suburbs
of Ohio. It wasn't because of the Shakers
or the headstones. It wasn't because
of the bloodless deaths we had seen
in movies or the everyday funerals
for birds & tadpoles & insects
we took apart like windup clocks & never
could put back together. We were so young
the cycles of nature evoked more wonder
than trepidation. Skulls found in the woods
were miracles to be held, to rub clean
& turn over, more exciting than finding
a magic lamp. The world beckoned & sang
to us without electricity. On that grassy hill
in the Shaker cemetery behind my house,
we lay on our backs staring longer than ever
at cloud shapes moving & re-forming over us.
Love I didn't recognize, but now I know it was
the first time I was conscious of the sky
never beginning & never ending.

Time

Scratched into the surface
of what were about to become slate sidewalk slabs,

the first dinosaur tracks were discovered
by James Deane in 1835

in Greenfield, Mass, just up the road from Emily's
place where she was already

contemplating the universe.
My brother Dave, the Geologist, shouted from Bakersfield,

Cal when he found shark teeth
66 million years old. I reeled

in disbelief, picturing California
under water, picturing everything familiar

erased. Pure emptiness & space
so ancient that it makes

time feel like a feather. Picture lying
on your back on a summer night gazing

into the galaxies. Focus
on one bright star, call it earth, populate

it with nations the size of molecules
filled with cities & highways & malls.

Freeze. And then zoom back to earth to the US
to Massachusetts

to Amherst to the Homestead
on Main Street in the second-floor bedroom

to the pencil Emily Dickinson held
to write her poem about the lava step

created by a volcano 70 million
years before Dave's teeth. Did she plan

for the fascicles of her pencil scratchings
to compete with infinity?

Hitchcock created stone books, essentially
two fossil slates joined by a hinge

as permanent as the thread that stitched
together Emily's poems, her delicate

soul prints as astonishing as tail
feathers combed into prehistoric slate.

Ice & Fire

Once before Ben was born
I bought a copy of Philip Booth's *Available Light*
at Sherman's in Bar Harbor. I had no idea

what could grow out of frozen earth.
On that first long drive north, we sank
into a down comforter at Dale's outside Orono

where she kept the house at 50 degrees
in winter. I remember a heavy curtain
closing off the bedroom hallway & the surprise

of a hot water bottle between the sheets. Remember
when we stopped for gas, we had to leave the VW
Rabbit running so the starter wouldn't freeze?

And how the further north we drove, the less plowed
were the roads so that as long as we stayed inside
the icy tracks we could make it to Jean's in Aroostock?

When Jim dropped us off by snowmobile
at the unheated cabin, it took a while to start a fire
& thaw the pipes long enough to drink from the tap.

35 years later I'm standing outside Sherman's in July,
tugging a leash & not thinking about Booth
or the first flush of love, a long winter

drive or Ben as a young man. Not really
paying attention. "She must like my new ring,"
the woman with the arm-length tattoo said about

Jessie, our second Sheltie. I saw rings on every finger
but the one she meant was a diamond just minutes old.
The man on the bench beside her looked up & grinned.

Volver

First the toothbrush, & then her trademark
paper towels. My sister has a secret:

A year after her death, our mother has moved into
the third-floor guest room.

It's not as complicated as in Almódovar's movie
about murder & incest & fiery retribution.

Actually, quite simple.
Mom showed up after Diane's heart attack.

She understands the sudden jolt
into mortality. If there are reasons, they

are irrelevant. I haven't seen her, but Diane says
she's an easy guest: she eats little & entertains herself

studying photos & the closet-full of papers
none of us can throw out. Diane says you'll be shocked

at how normal it is to talk to her. Nothing is off limits,
but, she adds, nothing's resolved.

Small Talk

None of us spoke French or knew
sign language. No one had seen
more than three of the foreign films
up for an Oscar. In Finnish

Jessica mimed that she felt
more like the husband
whose life was ruined
than the wife who cheated

& ended up happily alone.
Someone quoted Leonard Cohen.
Someone who had just taken an online course
quoted Milosz. No one said

a word about the tanks approaching Kyiv
or the children buried in mass graves.
No one said it, but everyone
pictured Babi Yar. Howard

asked if we knew the Shostakovich
& everyone nodded
even though none of us did
& in the kitchen

after the kettle boiled
& the deli platter was unwrapped,
everyone lined up with paper plates
& started talking at once.

Believe It

on the anniversary of the Tree of Life shooting

When 11 Jews were murdered in Pittsburgh
I was sitting in shul, as they were, studying Torah,

reading about the terror of Noah but not really
believing in world-destroying floods & thinking anyone

who says he hears God would be classified a fool,
not a prophet. Anyone who cries I want to kill all the Jews

as the police are carrying him out of a temple where he
has murdered 11 worshipers on Shabbat has got to be

mad. When I walked by the Tree of Life in the 1980s
on the way to see my love in Shadyside, I never paid attention

to the voices praying & never questioned how safe
I felt in Squirrel Hill, so Jewish even the Giant Eagle Supermarket

felt haimish. No one checked IDs or expected to see security cams
in a sanctuary. No one questioned what it meant to welcome

the stranger. Life between the Allegheny & the Monongahela
felt pretty grand, but don't forget how in 1936

flood waters rose 46 feet in downtown Pittsburgh
before a dam was conceived. Who was listening then?

Lightning Sonnet

For 40 years it's been a story
they keep inside until meeting
someone else who was there & then
they share the tale over & over:

how the wet grass
held the shape of the boys' bodies,
how purple & bloated their faces were
after they were carried inside & then

the twin funerals & now
how connected everyone feels
but grayer & still angry with
or in some cases closer to

God, their adult children's children
the same age as the boys.

Lee Road Accident

They said there was a boy on a bike
which translated to a boy flying over the hood
of a car, but to a child's mind
the image was more animated
than real. The logic went: I am safe
because they are safe, so he must be safe.

But the parts beyond our experience—the parts
where there were no words & thus no images
—went unremembered. Even stranger
was my mother's silence & my misreading
her calm. (Sometimes we'd think her screams
over a burnt steak were a coronary.)

Fifty years later, as I slow for a stop sign on Lee Road,
my father points out the house where the boy lived
& the intersection where he lost his life. Here?
He died? He came out of nowhere
on his bike before the light changed & the car
in the other direction hit him full on.

This isn't the story I thought I knew.
My parents must have heard the sounds
of metal crushing bone before they leapt from their car.
My father must have felt the boy shiver when he held him
wrapped in his coat until his parents, who lived
across the street, came running down their drive.

My mother and Lenore must have held each other
and wept, long after the ambulance arrived.
Even before it was reported, they must have known.
They had to know the boy would die.
I looked at my father, calm, beside me.
And I thought of that little boy and his parents.

I thought about what it must have felt like
to make the long walk back to their house,
how impossible to erase the images and locate
the words. And then I thought of my mother
& her long history with illness & car accidents.
Even ten years after her death, I keep learning to revise.

Lockdown

The kids grow up on "Lockdown!
Lockdown! Lockdown!" shouted

without warning from a speaker
hidden over the bulletin board

in the back of the classroom. We
tack poems on the board & exemplary

student projects, amusing posters
of cats, and a few reminders

to Use Your Writing Process & Always
Say What You Think! Barricaded

behind desks & chairs, my students
ask if the new security guard carries a gun

& if the floor to ceiling windows are bulletproof.
Sometimes they sit silently. Sometimes they do

homework. Sometimes they tell stories
of mass shootings they remember

or what it was like in elementary
school when they could feel the terror

in adult voices. Some of them have secret
code words their families use in public

when they intuit a threat. They are used to
armed soldiers in Grand Central Station,

particularly at Christmas when the ticket
windows are lit with cheer, buskers

sing ecumenical ditties, & the city hums
with shoppers & travelers headed home.

Cross-Continental Calls

Before we're caught up
on Beachwood friends & the books
& concerts in the months since we last spoke, & even before
I can ask about Jann's first round of chemotherapy,

Gary asks how Betsy is doing
after her mother's death, & then abruptly he sings
Death Don't Have No Mercy, the Hot Tuna version he listens to
curled in his favorite chair for looking out on the streets of Seattle,

& without mentioning him, I realize he's still grieving
for Jacob & for all the children, everywhere,
who are taken too soon,
                           & later after writing
more drafts of the poem about Newtown & continuing

to struggle with Merwin's sense of gratitude,
I'm relearning how it's possible
to suffer loss and claim hope at the same time,
&, as always, it's not that one replaces the other,

but more that everything's tangled
& impossible to word, which might mean that to live
is both to accumulate grief & to be grateful for words,
for cross-continental calls, for songs.

Bread & Air

> *"One thing I ask of the Lord"* (Psalm 27)

The one thing I ask is to hear my son's voice
answer "nothing's new." He's in the kitchen

making soda bread, incubating ideas
for an essay, sipping a beer. The cat, KK,

rubs against his ankles while Old Crow Medicine Show
plays live on the antique turntable. He's a week

away from closed gyms and synagogues, empty classrooms
& long lines snaking down the aisles of Rite Aid

on the corner of Gallatin and Eastland Ave. That little bookstore
where I bought a Nashville cookbook will be locked. Kroger

open, but Pelican & Pig vacant & the Listening Room
will go silent. Someone takes a break from piling debris

in Five Points, about a mile south. In this moment, no one fears
the next tornado or the slashed tires the neighbors once found

around the back where they stack the recycling.
A little boy whistles on Petway. Another murmurs

in his sleep. A woman stirs lentil & curry soup
on the gas range. All is calm. They say the first to go

will be smell & taste. I know every caraway seed my son savors
in the bread he makes from his great-grandmother's recipe.

In County Clare, as she kneads dough on the farmhouse table,
she breathes in, she breathes out, & she sings a prayer.

God's Rules

In God's house, there's no room for obsession.
The kitchen sink gleams & the tap water

is uncontaminated. In God's house,
my mother, who walks bent over because

of osteoporosis, never has to stoop
to pick up a crumb from the kitchen floor.

She is untroubled by placemats slightly askew
& kitchen chairs not tucked perfectly under the table.

In God's house, no one fears death.
Our bodies age, but not in the bathroom mirror.

Masks are supplied in God's house, but optional. Disinfectant
is sprayed from the showers. Even the news, which seems to repeat,

is never threatening. In God's house, we sleep precisely
the same hours each night & work not for necessity

but for love. And there's always a kiss waiting at the door.
As long as they don't linger, guests are welcome in God's house

& their plates are never empty. We go to sleep in God's house
without stickiness from sex or inexhaustible heat waves.

There is no excrement. No need to recycle or compost
because there is no trash. Clouds are purely for wonder

above God's house, not a barrier to fly through when you're
in a hurry to see your grandkids. As a matter of fact,

the grandkids live downstairs in God's house.
They never touch the stove & they never make a mess.

Angels on Escalators

The closer to her end, the more
my mother believed in angels. She collected plaster

garden figures for the apartment porch &
reproductions of paintings of pudgy-faced white kids

with wings. Madonna & Child with Angels. This struck me
as very gentile. Besides Lot & Balaam or Jimmy

Stewart at Christmas, what did we know from angels?
& why, if my mother was dying, should I care if her angels

were Jewish? Not knowing who or what else to lean on,
she surrounded herself with winged strangers to increase

her chance of nearness to the divine.
When she sat bedside with others or read to the blind

she didn't expect that anyone—me?—would return
the kindness. When it was too hard to climb stairs,

she rode department store escalators in the slow lane
as angels hurried past her—ascending, descending—

just like in Jacob's dream. They were racing up & down
& she was going nowhere. Would you believe? Not even

eye contact. The ones who stayed past their shift wore baggy
blue nurses' garb, their wing bones pliant when hugged.

The Weight

Either he's lighter or I'm stronger
because it's no strain to carry

my father. I'm whispering
in his ear, rubbing his back,

pacing the room in soothing
rhythms, & then I'm in an airport

not knowing what time the plane
leaves for Paris or from which

gate. Ben & Betsy have already checked in
but I can't find them &, wouldn't you know,

the cell phone doesn't work. The attendants
couldn't be nicer when they toss

my bags into a locked bin but no one
can tell me when I'll depart.

My father, who once could lift two kids,
one in each arm, is becoming weightless

in his hospital gown. I'm beginning to think
that even if I can board a later flight,

I'll never find Ben & Betsy on the busy streets
of Paris. Yesterday, before I was carrying

so much grief, I learned that when Ida
swept in without warning, two lovers

drowned in their car trying to get home
after work. The car became light

as a broken tree branch. No riverbanks
or guardrails could contain the raging storm.

Here, nurses in their blue scrubs stare at screens
pulsing with precise times of arrival & departure.

Postcard from the Coast

Before Covid, you pushed at all the boundaries—
signing up for tours from assisted living, calling a cab
to take Louise to fancy dinners, riding your scooter
to water therapy & 3-hour Sabbath services entirely in Hebrew.

You drove & drove yourself until you no longer could. When I
arrived after not seeing you for a year & a half, you were bare-chested
& shrunken in a hospital bed. Eyes open but not responding.
You waited until I got there & then hung around for two days
listening with me to Stan Getz & Debbie Friedman,
holding hands & whispering, it's all right, it's all right.

Where I am writing this, I can hear seals moaning
across the bay. It sounds like they are howling in grief
but maybe that's my perception. Maybe they are claiming
their territory and announcing to the world that they are alive.

Jeffrey Schwartz discovered poetry in the downtown bookstores of Cleveland, Ohio. Politics and poetry steered him to Boston, where he completed two degrees, co-edited a literary magazine, and apprenticed in the rare book trade. In the 1980s, Schwartz completed a Doctor of Arts degree at Carnegie Mellon that combined rhetoric and creative writing. In summers, he and his wife, Betsy Bowen, worked at the Bread Loaf School of English where they helped create one of the first electronic networks to join teachers and students across the US.

Schwartz has been the recipient of a Connecticut Artist Fellowship and other awards. His first book was published by Alice James Books. More recently, his poems have appeared in *Hanging Loose, Paterson Literary Review, Pedestal Magazine, Naugatuck River Review,* the Berru Poetry Series sponsored by the Jewish Book Council, and elsewhere. *Picture Houses,* a hand-stitched, limited edition of poems on film, was published in 2018. In addition to poetry, Schwartz has written for books and journals on innovations in technology, film studies, interdisciplinary collaboration, and student-centered pedagogy, including his co-edited *Students Teaching, Teachers Learning*.

For 33 years, Schwartz taught English at Greenwich Academy, a PreK-12 girls school in Connecticut, where he helped establish a visiting writers' series, an annual Writers Festival, and an award-winning student magazine. He has also taught at a number of colleges and for Global Online Academy linking high school poets from around the world. Lately, he has worked with Jewish and interfaith organizations on social justice. Schwartz's wife and son are also English teachers and activists. They continue to be fascinated by the purposes of talk.

www.ingramcontent.com/pod-product-compliance
Lightning Source LLC
Chambersburg PA
CBHW022045080426
42734CB00009B/1250